EXPLORING
BUSINESS
AND
ECONOMICS

EXPLORING
BUSINESS
AND
ECONOMICS

Famous Financiers and Innovators

Norman L. Macht

Chelsea House Publishers
Philadelphia

Frontis: Henry Ford put America on wheels by creating an assembly line to produce cars cheap enough for the average family to afford. You could order one of these 1925 Fords in any color, as long as it was black. That was one way Ford kept the prices down.

CHELSEA HOUSE PUBLISHERS

EDITOR-IN-CHIEF Sally Cheney
DIRECTOR OF PRODUCTION Kim Shinners
PRODUCTION MANAGER Pamela Loos
ART DIRECTOR Sara Davis

Choptank Syndicate/Chestnut Productions

EDITORIAL Norman Macht and Mary Hull
PRODUCTION Lisa Hochstein
PICTURE RESEARCH Norman Macht

http://www.chelseahouse.com

First Printing

1 3 5 7 9 8 6 4 2

Library of Congress Cataloging-in-Publication Data

Macht, Norman L. (Norman Lee), 1929–
    Famous financiers and innovators / Norman Macht
    p. cm. – (Exploring business and economics)
    ISBN 0-7910-6637-1 (alk. paper)
1. Capitalists and financiers—Biography. I. Title. II. Series.
HG172.A2 M33 2001
332'.092'2—dc21   2001042507

Table of Contents

When Andrew Carnegie's company built the Brooklyn Bridge in 1883, it was the largest suspension bridge in the world and was considered a marvel of engineering and construction. The bridge still carries traffic between New York City and Brooklyn.

Big Visions and Small Details

ANDREW CARNEGIE

The prospects were bleak for 12-year-old Andrew Carnegie in the small town of Dunfermline, Scotland, in 1848. His father, Will, once a prosperous linen weaver, had been unable to compete with the new machine made fabrics of the Industrial Age. He was unemployed. The family had no money.

Fortunately, the Carnegies had relatives living in America. Hoping to improve their lives, the family borrowed the money for passage on a ship, crossed the Atlantic Ocean, and moved in with one of Andrew's aunts in a town across the Ohio River from Pittsburgh, Pennsylvania.

They needed income, so Andrew went to work, earning $1.20 a week in a textile factory. He had gone to school for only four years, but he had a keen mind, was eager to learn, observed everything, and forgot nothing. His energy and willingness to learn led him to better jobs. He went to school at night while working as a telegraph operator.

Andrew impressed one of his customers, the Pennsylvania Railroad, so much that they hired him. The railroad was a large, powerful business. Their freight and passenger trains rumbled over hundreds of miles of tracks in many states.

One day a train wreck occurred, stopping all traffic. Andrew was alone in the office. He believed he knew what should be done, but he had no authority to act. Aware that he could be fired for using his boss's name, he did it anyhow, telegraphing orders to the train crews. Soon the trains were rolling again. Instead of being fired, he was promoted.

Carnegie's Philanthropy

Andrew Carnegie believed that a rich man, having fulfilled the wants and needs of his family, should "consider all surplus revenues which come to him simply as trust funds which he is called upon to administer" and give away.

Cities and towns in the United States, Canada, Great Britain, and other English-speaking countries owe the start of their public library systems to Andrew Carnegie. Of the more than 2,500 libraries he built, 1,700 of them are in the United States. He endowed schools and universities. His foundations promote teaching and world peace, and, along with a fund that recognizes heroic acts by individuals, they continue to benefit society 100 years later. He also created a trust fund for Dunfermline, Scotland, the town where he was born.

The first railroads that spanned the country had to cross rivers and ravines. Sparks from the engines' smokestacks often set the wooden supports on fire, burning down the bridges. Andrew Carnegie made his first fortune by building bridges with iron supports instead of wood.

Andrew Carnegie had the soul of a born **entrepreneur.** Whatever he learned, he acted on. His curiosity enabled him to spot opportunities when they came along. He invested in a company that made railroad cars with seats that could be turned into beds for night travel. The company was successful. Soon the income from his investment was three times as much as his salary.

About that time the first oil well was drilled in western Pennsylvania. Andrew put his money into this booming new industry and became a rich man before he was 30. By 1863 his investment income was over $45,000 (equal to $600,000 today); his salary was only $2,400.

Andrew realized that it was more profitable to own a company than to work for one. He had grasped the essence of **capitalism:** an individual's right to take financial risks in hopes of gaining the rewards of success. He had seen railroad bridges made of wood catch fire from the hot embers that spewed out of locomotive smokestacks. So he started a company to make iron bridges, and soon had more projects than he could handle, including the famous Brooklyn Bridge. He knew that iron railroad tracks frequently broke or wore down and had to be replaced. When new methods were developed for making stronger and lighter steel, he understood that the new steel would enable the railroads to span the nation and tall skyscraper building to rise.

Andrew invested everything he had in iron and steel. He built new steel mills and bought others. He constantly modernized his equipment. If something new and better came along just a few months after he had installed new machines, he would throw out the new machines and put in newer ones.

But Andrew's main key to success was his attention to details. His competitors had no idea what it cost them to produce each ton of steel, but Andrew knew, to the penny. He was always looking for ways to cut costs. Cutting a half-cent off the cost of making a pound of steel added up to large profits when you were turning out 70,000 tons of rails for tracks.

He bought his own coal and iron mines, his own railroad lines for transport, and hired engineers to figure out ways to turn these raw materials into steel more efficiently. He was never satisfied; there was always a cheaper, better way to do the job and improve the product. His company became the biggest and lowest-cost steel producer in the country.

By 1890, when he was 55, Andrew Carnegie's annual income was the equivalent of about $40 million today. A decade later he sold it all to J. P. Morgan's United States Steel Corporation for $480 million (about $1 billion today).

Andrew Carnegie had become one of the richest men in the world by following the path he later advised for others: "I believe the true road to preeminent success in any line is to make yourself master in that line . . . My advice to young men would be not only to concentrate their whole time and attention on the one business in life in which they engage, but to put every dollar of their capital into it."

RAY KROC

Success is 10 percent inspiration, 90 percent perspiration. Ray Kroc didn't invent anything. He didn't improve anything. All he did was see something that inspired in him a vision. With that inspiration and a lot of hard work, he created something that has become a part of everyday life in thousands of cities and towns in 120 countries.

Born in Chicago in 1902, Ray Kroc wanted to be a piano player. But he wasn't a very good piano player. He soon learned that there were a lot of people who were better than he was. If he wanted to earn a living, he had to find another line of work.

For a while he tried selling Florida real estate. In 1927 he became a salesman for a paper cup company. The common Styrofoam cups of today had just been introduced. Business was good. Unlike millions of other workers, Ray kept his job through the Depression years of the 1930s, a time when many people were out of work and had no money.

One of his customers, who owned an ice cream shop, had invented a milk shake mixer, called a Multimixer, that could churn five big shakes at the same time. He and Ray formed a partnership, and Ray began selling the Multimixers to ice cream stands like Dairy Queen that were springing up all over the country in the 1940s after World War II.

Ray Kroc's territory covered the entire country. He did a lot of traveling, selling one machine at a time to hamburger stands and ice cream shops in small rural towns. One day in 1954 he called on a hamburger stand in San Bernardino, a small town located amid the remote canyons and mountains of southern California. He was astonished when the owners, two brothers named Mac and Dick McDonald, ordered eight Multimixers. How could a little stand do so much business that they needed enough machines to make 40 milkshakes at one time?

Ray hung around to find out. He spoke to customers in the parking lot and watched them devour the hamburgers as if they hadn't eaten for a week. He saw a steady stream of fries going out of the drive-in window at 10 cents a bag like a never-ending gusher pouring out of a broken pipe.

Inside, he studied the brothers as they flipped burgers and put them on buns with the precision of an army drill team. The fries operation was equally fine-tuned down to the smallest detail.

Ray stayed in town long enough to learn the McDonald brothers' secrets: insistence on the highest quality materials, quality control and efficiency at every step of the process, and close attention to details. He learned what kind of potatoes they bought, and how they stored and washed and peeled and sliced and fried them. He noticed that they never used the french fry oil to cook anything else. He watched them measure the fat content of the beef, the shape of the burgers, the cooking time.

At night Ray lay awake imagining what it would be like if he could duplicate the McDonald brothers' operation in hundreds, maybe even thousands, of towns. The more he thought about it, the more determined he became to make it happen.

The brothers had thought about opening a few more stands themselves, but they were making more money than they could spend already. Ray wasn't. The Multimixer business was not going well. Kroc needed something new to sell.

Ray Kroc was a salesman. He sold the brothers on letting him sell **franchises** to people to copy the brothers' way of doing business. The brothers insisted that the initial franchise fee be low; Ray would earn his money by getting a percentage of the franchisees' revenues. His income would depend on how well they did. This gave Ray the incentive to work hard to make every McDonald's restaurant a success.

Ray spread the brothers' standards and methods to every part of the country, with unbending insistence on quality, and fanatic attention to details. Every beef patty had to be the same size with the same fat content. He studied hamburger buns by the hour before settling on the right size and shape and texture. If he visited a McDonald's and it wasn't

Big Macs Around the World

In 1965 Ray Kroc opened up McDonald's to public investors, and the company has been a popular investment as well as eating place ever since.

As of 2001, there were 28,000 McDonald's in 120 countries. Most of the company's profits came from outside the United States. Not every McDonald's in the world looks the same or has the same menu. The chain adapts its menus in other countries to suit the tastes and habits of the people they are serving, and sometimes has to conform to the architecture of the area, especially in ancient towns visited by tourists.

This promotion, sponsored by a McDonald's in Germany, centered on the Olympic Games. Overseas McDonald's often vary their offerings to accommodate foreign tastes.

clean enough to suit him, he would grab a mop and show the manager how it should be done.

Ray's goal was to insure that customers could depend on everything being the same wherever they went into a McDonald's. He set up a training center near Chicago,

Illinois, called Hamburger University; new franchise holders took a three-week course in the McDonald's methods. Today millions of youngsters still get their first jobs at a McDonald's.

Ray resented that he was doing all the work and back in San Bernardino the McDonald brothers were getting rich. After angry negotiations he bought them out, taking the name with him. Ray never thought anything but big and bigger. After five years he had 250 McDonald's scattered across the country. That was just the beginning. A decade later he was opening almost that many every year. He introduced new products. Some, like the Big Mac, succeeded. Others, like the Hulaburger, flopped. But the fries kept marching out under the chain's trademark golden arches.

This drawing of the celebrated Mickey Mouse, the symbol of the Walt Disney Company, first appeared in the 1939 animated film *The Pointer.*

Swim Your Own Race

WALT DISNEY

Geniuses are born, not made. Education and training can help them improve their skills, but no amount of schooling can transform somebody into a creative, original thinker or artist.

Walt Disney was born with a gift in Chicago in 1901. When he was four, the family moved to a farm in Missouri. For the next four years Walt played with the farm animals, and roamed the nearby woods looking for rabbits, raccoons, and other forest dwellers that would later appear in his work.

He already had the urge to draw pictures. But his first effort earned him no praise. Walt found some tar, dipped a stick into it, and drew a picture on the side of their white house. His father, a stern man who considered drawing pictures a waste of time, was not amused. When Walt stuck to crayons on paper his work was better received.

Walt did not begin school until he was seven. His father did not want him to go to school until his younger sister was ready, so Walt was seven when he entered first grade. He was never much of a student, preferring to doodle on his test papers. He drew faces and animals on pads of paper that he would then flip with his thumb, creating the appearance of moving figures.

When Walt was eight, his family moved to Kansas City. His father put him to work delivering newspapers in the predawn hours. Walt enjoyed visiting the home of a friend, whose father was a jolly jokester, unlike his own father. The friend's family took Walt to see his first motion pictures, silent films starring the comic genius Charlie Chaplin.

Walt was a good mimic. He enjoyed copying Chaplin's antics and portraying such historic figures as Abraham Lincoln in pageants. He loved to read, but not textbooks. He repeated the second grade and was 16 by the time he got out of the eighth grade. He preferred reading the works of storytellers like Mark Twain and Charles Dickens.

The family moved to Chicago where Walt drew cartoons for the school magazine and went to art school three nights a week. At 17 he dropped out of school. After his two older brothers went into the service during World War I, he signed up for the Red Cross Ambulance Corps. While in France as a driver, he decorated ambulances, trucks, jackets, and helmets with his cartoon characters.

When the war ended in 1918, Walt went to Kansas City, where his brother Roy worked in a bank. Though he enjoyed the movies, Walt saw no place in them for an artist.

Walt Disney examines some film while Mickey Mouse looks on. Born in Disney's imagination in 1928, Mickey Mouse built the foundation for the world of Disney, and Mickey remains the world's most famous rodent.

His ambition was to be a political cartoonist for a newspaper. But he could not get a job. He worked for a short time at a commercial art company, where he met another young artist named Ub Iwerks. Together they moved to a company that made one-minute animated commercials to be shown in movie theaters. All thoughts of becoming a political cartoonist vanished.

Walt plunged into the study of drawing characters and photographing them one picture at a time to create the appearance of movement. He bought a camera and produced short cartoons in his own workshop and sold them to local theaters. For six months he worked on a longer cartoon he hoped to sell to start his own business. When it was finished he quit his job. He was 20.

Walt persuaded some investors to put up the money to form a company called Laugh-O-gram Films. A distributor bought six of his cartoons, but never paid for them. Disney and Laugh-O-gram were broke.

Walt's brother urged him to forget cartoons and get a steady job, but he refused to give up his dreams. Believing his only chance to work in movies was in live-action films, Walt headed for Hollywood in 1923, where he had an uncle he could live with until he found a job.

For two months Walt knocked on doors with no luck. His brother Roy then suggested that he go back to his first love, drawing cartoons. The brothers borrowed $500 from their uncle, rented a store, and turned it into Disney Brothers Studio. They made and sold three **animated cartoons.** The cartoons were good, but Walt's business methods were bad. The distributor failed to pay the full amount they had agreed on. Expenses went up and income went down.

Walt realized that there were better artists in Hollywood than he was. One was his old friend, Ub Iwerks, who came to California to work with him. They hired a few others, and Walt Disney stopped drawing and began to focus on his true talent: creating ideas, stories, and characters, and supervising their production. His first star was Oswald the Lucky Rabbit.

Geniuses can be perfectionists, driven to working long hours to achieve perfection. That can make them hard to work for, as they often demand the same dedication and discipline from the people who work for them. When his distributor opened a competing studio and lured away most of his workers, they did not hesitate to leave him, taking the rights to Oswald with them. Disney had to start over again.

Mickey Mouse, Walt said later, just popped out of his mind. He had enjoyed watching tiny mice flitting about in his wastebasket when he worked late at night back in Kansas City. He had just enough money to turn out three Mickey Mouse cartoons. The last was his first cartoon with sound, in 1928. Mickey was an instant hit.

Now more than 70 years old, Mickey Mouse, the most famous rodent in the world, was the foundation for everything to come in the wonderland created by Walt Disney: including the first full-length animated feature, *Snow White and the Seven Dwarfs,* in 1937; Donald Duck, Goofy, Pluto, Dumbo, Bambi, and the entire menagerie of Disney characters; motion pictures; television shows; Disneylands in California, Japan, and Europe; and Walt Disney World in Florida.

TED TURNER

If ever a man followed Andrew Carnegie's advice about sticking to one business and putting all your money into it, that man was R. E. "Ted" Turner III. A fearless risk-taker

The Empire That Walt Disney Created

Walt Disney died of lung cancer on December 15, 1966. He was recognized as a genius of innovation and ideas in his field. Until his last day he was still supervising a new attraction for Disneyland, which had opened in 1955, and outlining in his imagination Walt Disney World, which would open five years after his death.

Today the Walt Disney Company has grown far beyond even its founder's imagination. The company owns the Anaheim Angels baseball team, the Mighty Ducks of Anaheim hockey team, television networks such as ABC, ESPN, A&E, and the History Channel, and movie, record and book publishing interests, vacation clubs, and a cruise line.

Ted Turner did things his own way, took big risks, spoke his mind, fought giant corporations, earned plenty of enemies, and changed the way television covered the news of the world. Like Andrew Carnegie, he then began giving away some of the billions of dollars he had made.

who turned his associates into nervous wrecks with his financial gambles, Ted Turner not only risked his own money, he borrowed heavily to back his bets. His business was selling advertising, and in the process he revolution-ized the television industry and changed the world.

Ted Turner's story is not a rags-to-riches tale. Born November 29, 1938, in Cincinnati, Ted attended Brown University, where he was active in debating and yachting. When he was 24 his father died. Ted inherited the family business: billboards for which they sold advertising.

Ted was smart, impetuous, and creative; conservative businessmen called him crazy. Based in Atlanta, he built his billboard business into the biggest in the south. But that was only the beginning. There were other ways to sell advertising—radio, for instance. Ted set out to buy a radio station. He found one he liked that was for sale. He went home and thought about it. While he was thinking, somebody else came along and bought it. Later, when he got around to buying the station, it cost him a lot more money. That taught him a lesson: follow your instincts and act quickly on them.

Ted bought more radio stations and, in 1970, he bought a struggling little Atlanta television station that nobody watched. The station was losing money and he knew nothing about the television business. That didn't stop him. If he could sell commercials, he would learn the rest.

At that time there were only five TV stations in Atlanta. When one went out of business, Ted proudly declared that his station had moved up from fifth to fourth in the market. He ran the cheapest programming he could find, mostly old sitcoms and movies, but the station still lost money.

National TV networks used expensive telephone lines on microwave relay towers to transmit their signals across the country. In 1976 satellites were launched that could do the same thing. Ted Turner decided that was the way to go. He didn't care that a satellite hookup would cost almost a million dollars. He called the company and ordered one, while his bookkeepers turned pale. He didn't have the money.

Overnight, like Cinderella, on December 17, 1976, his tiny TV station in Atlanta turned into a national superstation. With the spread of cable systems, it could now be seen in millions of homes all over America.

To fill the broadcast time on his station, Ted bought hundreds of old movies. He bought the rights to the Atlanta Braves baseball games. The Braves were a terrible team in the 1970s, but he didn't care. The games filled a lot of time on his station during the six-month season. He could now offer a national audience to sponsors. When the Braves were put up for sale, Ted bought the team to keep the TV rights.

Until now, Ted had devoted very little time to news programs on his superstation. The major networks spent millions of dollars on news staffs and star anchors. He couldn't compete with them, and didn't try. He saw a different—and better—way to get into the news business. He would create an all-news 24-hour TV station and rely on local reporters in cities all over the world. His schedule would not be locked into specific news times. Any time something was happening anywhere in the world—wars, earthquakes, speeches, fires, strikes, riots—whatever would make the network evening news, he would show it live while it was happening. For the first time people could witness the events of the world, scheduled and unscheduled.

The project lost more than $2 million a month in the first year, but Cable News Network (CNN), which went on the air on June 1, 1980, was here to stay. On CNN, leaders spoke directly to millions of people, not through interviews that would be edited and shown hours or days later. The world watched riots in China and Moscow on CNN. CNN covered the Persian Gulf War live in 1990–91. Other networks, world leaders, and the public watched it on television just as spectators had once gathered on hillsides outside Washington to watch Civil War battles. CNN was seen in 89 countries and was hugely profitable.

No game was too big for Ted Turner, who had been dubbed "the Mouth of the South" by his envious competitors, who saw him as a brash, outspoken upstart. He showed up at high-level meetings wearing cowboy boots and chewed tobacco while other corporate types wore their blue suits and ties.

Ted's broadcasting empire made a lot of money, but it was built on a lot of debt. He had more ideas for growth but was short of cash. So he merged his company with the rich communications giant, Time Warner, an empire of movie studios, magazines, TV stations, and cable networks. The deal made him a billionaire, Time Warner's biggest stockholder with 11 percent of the **stock.** But he was no longer in charge.

That didn't stop Ted Turner. He let them know he was still around, voicing his opinions when he didn't like something. He took on other media giants, said whatever was on his mind, and didn't care if it made somebody mad. He had always been one to swim his own race and he saw no need to change.

In 2000 Time Warner merged with the Internet service America Online to form a gigantic international communications company. Ted Turner's presence became smaller as the company grew bigger. At 62, he was a multibillionaire. But after 40 years of building and running his own company he was now, he said, "sitting at the end of the hallway with nothing to do."

SEARS, ROEBUCK AND CO.

INCORPORATED

CHEAPEST SUPPLY HOUSE

AUTHORIZED
AND
INCORPORATED
UNDER THE LAWS
OF
ILLINOIS

ON EARTH.
OUR TRADE REACHES AROUND
THE WORLD.

WITH A CAPITAL
OF
$150.000.00
PAID IN FULL

REFERENCE BY
SPECIAL PERMISSION
NAT'L BANK OF THE REPUBLIC CHICAGO
METROPOLITAN NAT'L BANK   "
NAT'L BANK OF ILLINOIS   "
GERMAN EXCHANGE BANK NEW YORK

CONSUMERS GUIDE

CATALOGUE
No 105

82 to 96 FULTON
73 to 87 DESPLAINES
and 17 to 31 WAYMAN STREET
CHICAGO, ILL. U.S.A.

Before the days of malls and automobiles, the arrival in the mail of the Sears, Roebuck catalog was an exciting event in the lives of millions of people throughout the country. Called the wish book, the catalog offered for sale just about everything anybody could want or need.

The Peddlers

RICHARD W. SEARS

America was a nation of farmers when Richard W. Sears was born in Minnesota in 1863. Eighty percent of the population lived in the country or in small towns, only 20 percent lived in cities.

When farmers needed supplies from a store, they hitched up a wagon and drove into the nearest town to the general store. There they stocked up on everything from shirts and shoes to sugar and flour. Their wives brought home sewing and dress-making materials. Larger items, like wood-burning stoves and parlor pianos, could be bought from mail-order houses, which shipped the goods by the railroads that were rapidly connecting cities and towns in all directions.

The storekeepers ordered their goods by mail or from traveling salesmen, called drummers, who went from town to town taking orders for the products they represented.

Richard Sears was a born trader. He studied the pamphlets and advertisements for all kinds of things and bought whatever he could trade with other boys for something better or sell for a few cents more than he had paid for it.

At 15 he became a telegraph operator for the railroad. He was soon promoted to station agent in North Redwood, Minnesota. In that job he handled all the freight that people ordered from the cities in the east. He studied every page of the **catalogs** that came across his desk: the goods they offered, the prices they charged. He compared the prices of the same goods from different companies, and calculated the amount of profit in each item.

One day in 1886 a shipment of gold-filled pocket watches from Chicago arrived at the North Redwood station. The only jeweler in the area said he hadn't ordered them and didn't want them. When Richard notified the company that the watches were unclaimed, they said if he wanted them, he could buy them for $12 each. The popular watches sold for $25 in the stores. Richard saw an opportunity to make some money and took it. He started clicking his telegraph key to the other station agents along the line, offering them $25 watches for $14. He sold them all.

Richard became a pocket watch agent on the side, selling them to other agents who in turn sold the watches for a few dollars more to customers in their own towns. In less than a year he had accumulated $5,000 in profits, equal to $95,000 today. He quit his job and started his own business, the R. W. Sears Watch Company.

The era of the Sears catalog is over; these days Sears customers may choose to shop online. Online shopping is the most radical development in the retail industry since Richard Sears developed his extensive catalog.

Richard Scars had a way with words. He was a natural pitchman, someone who rattles off a sales pitch exaggerating the virtues of whatever he's selling. He moved to Chicago and began placing his effusive adds in the newspapers, offering watches for less than the stores charged. Business was so good, he began to get letters asking if he could repair watches, too. Richard knew nothing about repairing watches. But he knew a chance to make money when he saw it. He advertised for an expert watch repairman, and hired Alvah C. Roebuck.

A year later, restless again, Richard sold the business for the equivalent of more than a million dollars today. He was rich, but he was only 26. He started another business, still selling watches, and took Roebuck in as a partner. In 1891 they published a 52-page catalog of nothing but watches. The next year they doubled its size and added other jewelry and accessories, including revolvers. The following year they added clothing, pianos, organs, and sewing machines.

In 1893 they incorporated as Sears, Roebuck & Company, and published the first of the thick, all-inclusive catalogs that became the most widely read annual publication in the country. Richard had earned the confidence and trust of farmers everywhere. They were no longer at the mercy of the local general store. Sear's prices were lower, the quality of his goods better, and the Sears offer of guaranteed satisfaction was dependable.

As the rural areas prospered along with the cities, their buying power grew. Because of his background, Richard Sears knew farmers—what they wanted and needed, and

A Mail Order Man

Many successful businesses have begun when someone with imagination saw a need that was not being met, or found a way to do something better and cheaper than anyone else. When Richard W. Sears died in 1914, *Printer's Ink,* an advertising magazine wrote:

"R. W. Sears was a mail-order man, had the mail-order viewpoint, knew how to use advertising space, knew the value of copy, knew the conditions surrounding mail-order publications, and he succeeded in a big way because he possessed those qualities to a greater degree than any other mail-order man who ever lived."

how they thought. The dynamic language he used to promote the use of his catalogs whetted the customers' appetite so much that they couldn't wait to send for one. In 1897 they sold 318,000 catalogs.

The Sears, Roebuck catalog became known as the wish book, the farmer's friend. It enabled families who lived miles away from their nearest neighbor, and hundreds of miles from a city, to own and enjoy the same worldly goods as city dwellers. The books were profusely illustrated. Sold for as much as 50 cents at first, by 1904 they were given away. For millions of families, waiting for a package from Sears to arrive was a source of excitement: a boy's baseball glove, a girl's new dress, new furniture for the parlor, a man's new radio, a woman's new hat and shoes.

Four times a year 15 million catalogs went out in the mail. They grew to over 1,500 pages offering 70,000 items. Its place in American history and nostalgia is reflected in the popularity of reprints of the old catalogs that are sold today.

Sears also opened retail stores and centers where people could come in and order from the catalogs. The company became the biggest retailer in the world and remained at the top until Wal-Mart passed it.

In recent years catalog companies have multiplied dramatically, to the dismay of mail carriers who have to deliver them, especially during the month before Christmas. Of the hundreds of catalogs stuffed into mailboxes every day, the Sears, Roebuck catalog is no longer among them. It was last distributed in 1993.

SAM WALTON

An idea doesn't have to be complicated to be good. It doesn't even have to be original. But if it's going to amount

Sam Walton didn't invent anything. He just worked harder and longer hours and smarter than his competitors, until he had built the largest retail business in the world. It also made him the richest man, not only in his home town of Bentonville, Arkansas, but the entire country.

to anything, it has to be followed by a willingness to stick to it despite obstacles and setbacks, and to put in years of long hours and hard work.

Sam Walton had a simple idea: open a store, buy merchandise at low prices, and sell it at low prices. He believed that if you could buy a lot of stuff for a dollar and sell it for two, you'd be more successful if you sold it for $1.50 instead. Walton wasn't thinking small; he never thought small. Give customers a bargain and they'll come back, he reasoned. A lot of small profits would make him more money than a few big ones.

Sticking to that idea made Sam Walton the richest man in America when he died in 1992. But becoming a multibillionaire never changed him. He was still living in a modest house in Bentonville, Arkansas, a town of 10,000, where he had opened his first store, still driving an old pickup truck, working out of an office about the size of an average bedroom. He did own an airplane—and flew it himself mainly because it was quicker than driving the curving mountain roads to go quail hunting or visit his stores.

Sam Walton was born on a farm near Kingfisher, Oklahoma, on March 29, 1918. When he was five, the family left the failing farm and moved to another small town in Missouri. His father preached hard work and practiced it. His industrious example took root in Sam, who studied hard, played sports, pursued Eagle Scout honors, and did odd jobs. Sam kept up that active pace all his life. He was quiet, soft-spoken, polite, and led by the example of how much honest effort he put into everything he did. In his senior year in high school the family moved to Colombia, Missouri. He was elected president of the student body, even though he was a new kid in town.

Sam graduated from the University of Missouri, just a few blocks from the Walton home, in 1940. He took a job as a trainee with the J. C. Penney Company, then one of the largest retail chains in the country, with 1,586 stores, mostly in small towns.

The lessons he learned there became his own business philosophy: customer satisfaction; small price **markups;** square deals; considerate treatment of employees. Penney's called its employees associates; Sam Walton later did the same.

After his army service during World War II, Sam Walton, now married and a father, bought a 5-and-10-cent store in the Ben Franklin chain in Newport, Arkansas. Ben Franklin stores sold a variety of inexpensive merchandise. There weren't more than 4,000 people in the remote town of Newport. That suited Sam Walton fine; he was, and would always be, a small-town man. And the fishing and hunting were good.

In those days 5-and-10 stores actually sold a wide variety of merchandise for as little as a nickel or dime. The store prospered and Sam became active in civic affairs, serving as president of the Chamber of Commerce. There was nothing high-hat about Sam. The people in Newport called him "common as anybody," their highest compliment. He was always smartly dressed and always busy. Normally easy-going, he became angry only when someone failed to keep his word with him.

When he wasn't in the front of the store greeting cus-tomers, Sam was studying the huge flow of new products coming onto the market after the war. He installed ice cream and popcorn machines and had customers lined up on Saturday afternoons when the farmers came to town.

Sam's store was so successful that when his lease was up, the property owner would not renew it. He wanted the store for one of his sons. Just like that, Sam Walton was out of business. He was still full of energy, optimism, and the drive to be the leader wherever he landed.

That turned out to be an even smaller town—Bentonville—where he bought a dirty, rundown store and sank all his money into remodeling and expanding it. The store pros-pered from the start, and Sam got to thinking: if he could run one store, why not two? Joined by his brother, he opened a second store in a town 25 miles away.

In the early 1950s the shopping center was a new concept. The second one in the country opened in Kansas City, Missouri, in 1953, and Sam Walton had a store in it. It proved so successful, he envisioned shopping centers going up all over the country, and he decided that he would build them. But when he ran out of money on his first project, he went back to the business he knew—variety stores.

Sam Walton had a nose for everything: hot items that would sell, good store managers, and good locations. He was always looking, always thinking, weighing everything he saw, and working long hours. He didn't mind getting down on his knees and putting down floor tiles or carrying merchandise from one store to another. He went into his competitors' stores and took notes about what he saw, what they were doing better than he was, and asked a lot of questions.

A Man of the People

Sam Walton's management style is called "management by walking around." To him, this meant being constantly on the move, checking out his own and competitors' stores, getting to know the associates in his stores, and motivating them, listening and learning, noticing everything—instead of sitting in a big fancy office and never being seen by the people working for him. His buyers of merchandise drove the hardest deals in the business, and passed the savings to the customers.

Frugality was also his style, in both business and personal life. At one time the richest man in America, Sam Walton spent little money on himself, but wanted nothing. Corporate headquarters were as stark as a bus station. He dressed and traveled and entertained no better than his average employee.

Wal-Mart Stores, Inc.

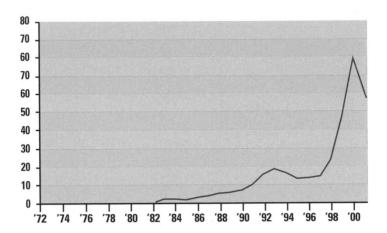

Wal-Mart employees who invested in the company became millionaires as a result of the growth of the stock in the past 20 years.

And he had big dreams. Soon he owned a dozed Ben Franklin stores. He opened the biggest stores anybody had ever seen in little towns of 2,000 and 3,000 people. Working from the early morning to late at night, he found sources of merchandise at bargain prices which he then sold at bargain prices.

The K-Mart chain of discount stores, launched in 1962, was growing rapidly. By 1966 they would be doing $1 billion in annual sales. Sam Walton saw its potential. Unable to persuade the Ben Franklin officials to follow his lead, Walton set out on his own. In 1962 he leased a new building in Rogers, Arkansas, and opened the first Wal-Mart. It was soon followed by another, then another—all in small sleepy towns where Wal-Mart became the biggest thing in town.

To keep up with the growing business, Sam had to design new ways to buy, warehouse, and deliver merchandise, always with an eye to cutting costs. All that took more money than he had. Walton found an insurance company that would lend him $2.5 million. He raised more by going public, selling stock in the company to the public for the first time. People who invested $2,000 in Wal-Mart in 1970 and kept the stock became millionaires within 20 years.

Walton used the money to expand to five states. They had 50 stores and kept growing. The rest is history. By 2001 Wal-Mart was the biggest retailer in the world, with more than 1,700 stores, 300 superstores, and about 500 discount stores, known as Sam's Clubs, in the United States, and 1,100 stores in Latin America, Europe, Canada, and Asia.

Sam Walton's dream had never been to amass a lot of wealth. It had been to become the number one retailer in America. That dream did not just come true. Sam Walton made it happen.

Always interested in saving the consumer money, Henry Ford looked for ways to cut costs. When parts were shipped to his factories on wooden pallets, Ford recycled the pallets and put the wood on the sides of the first "woodies," or wood-sided cars.

Building a Better Mousetrap

HENRY FORD

"Build a better mousetrap, and the world will beat a path to your door." This old proverb reminds us that finding a better way to make something can lead to success as much as inventing something.

Henry Ford didn't invent the automobile, or the gasoline engine. He wasn't even the first automobile manufacturer. What he did was find a way to manufacture cars cheaply enough to bring them within the reach of millions of Americans. More than anyone else, Henry Ford was responsible for creating a nation on wheels.

Before the invention of the gasoline engine, cars were powered by steam, which was impractical. Drivers frequently ran out of fuel before they reached their destinations.

Henry Ford was born on a farm near Detroit on July 30, 1863. There were plenty of chores to do, tending animals and orchards and vegetable gardens, sowing and reaping the crops. Though he had to pitch in and do his share, only one thing on the farm really interested Henry: the McCormick mechanical reaper. At harvest time this horse-drawn mechanism could do the work of 10 men. This was his thing. He liked nothing better than to be told that the machinery needed fixing.

Henry loved to take things apart to see what made them work. Nothing was safe from his curiosity. When he was 13 he fixed a friend's broken pocket watch, making the tools he needed. About that time he saw his first steam-powered farm machine. That opened a fascinating new world of interest for him.

Unknown to Henry, steam-powered vehicles had been around a long time. The first such tractor made its debut in France in 1770, moving at a speed of three miles an hour. Noisy, smoking steam carriages and buses were common in England in the 1800s. By the 1890s more than 100 models of steam cars would be made in America.

A steam-powered vehicle was not easy to operate. It had to carry a tank filled with water, a burner to heat the water, and a box to hold the wood or coal to keep the fire going. The operator frequently ran out of water or fuel.

When he was 16 Henry had enough of school—he never went past the eighth grade—and the family farm. He went to Detroit to work at various jobs where there was machinery—lots of machines of all kinds. That was all he wanted to learn about. After three years he returned to the farm, but he didn't do any farming. He built a machine shop and worked at repairing steam engines for farmers in the surrounding countryside.

Like other mechanics, Henry realized that, if the automobile had a future, electric and gasoline engines would have to replace steam. In 1899 he went to work for the Detroit electric company, where he learned everything he could about this new energy source. Electricity was still experimental; the light bulb was not invented until 1893. On his own time, Henry built a gas buggy in his garage, making all the parts by hand. It took him three years. When it was finished he discovered that it wouldn't fit through the garage door. He had to cut a hole in the wall to get his invention out.

On a rainy Thursday night, June 4, 1896, he started it up and drove his first horseless carriage out onto a Detroit street. The buggy was no more that a box on four bicycle wheels. It had no brakes. But it worked.

In 1885, German mechanics had been the first to build the kind of gasoline engine used today. Other mechanics were now building gas-powered cars in Detroit. But the horseless carriage was considered a rich man's toy and nothing more. That was partly because building a car by hand was slow, and the auto companies could not make many. So they were very expensive, costing thousands of dollars at a time when the average working man earned about $500 a year.

The motorcars that were on the road were noisy and smelly. The public did not like them. They scared horses and bicycle riders, threatened pedestrians, ran into fences and trees. Nobody knew how to drive one when they bought it.

The automobile manufacturing industry grew slowly without Henry Ford. Year after year he continued to work on perfecting his machines. Every time he found investors to back him, he lost them because he never produced any

The Model T

The Model T Ford, also called the Tin Lizzie, made Henry Ford the most successful businessman of his time. He produced 15 million of them between 1906 and 1927, a period when more than half the cars sold in America were Fords. He kept the price down by standardizing and streamlining production. It took 90 minutes to put together all but the body of a car in 1913.

Henry Ford controlled everything he needed to produce his automobiles, from the coal and iron ore used to make the steel to the railroad that carried his cars to market. Here iron ore is being loaded onto a barge on Lake Superior to be transported to the Ford steel mills in Detroit.

automobiles to sell. He built two racing cars, both winners, but nothing to sell to the public.

By the time he was satisfied that he had perfected something he could offer for sale, most of the wealthy men in Detroit wanted nothing more to do with him. They considered him a poor business risk. Unable to raise the money to build a factory, Henry had to settle for buying the parts from other machine shops and assembling them in his own shop.

Henry Ford was 40 years old when he sold his first automobile, called Model A. It was an immediate success. The Ford Motor Company sold 650 of them in 1903. For the first time Ford's backers were happy. They urged him to make a new model every year, each one fancier and more expensive and profitable. Everybody was happy except Henry Ford. He had a different vision.

Henry saw the motor car as a useful everyday machine for everyone, instead of a rich man's toy. He was determined to design one that was dependable, easily repaired, would last for years, and was cheap. If he could lower the cost of building it, he would lower the price to make it affordable to the average working man.

Until now, Henry Ford had done nothing different from 100 other auto manufacturers. From now on, he would do things differently. And every time he did, people said he was crazy. That never stopped him.

Beginning in 1908, Henry Ford:
- designed the Model T, his basic "Everyman's" car, which remained in production for 18 years
- built the largest automobile plant in the world to make his cars
- lowered the price of the automobile, from $950 in 1909 to $490 in 1913 (equal to $8,500 today)
- paid his workers $5 a day, double the going rate, for an eight-hour day, to attract and keep the best employees
- introduced programs to improve his employees' living conditions
- created the modern **assembly line;** conveyors brought parts to workers who added them to the vehicles that passed in front of them on continuous conveyor belts
- created the first all-inclusive industrial plant in the world's largest factory, the River Rouge plant in Michigan.

By 1927 Henry owned his own coal and iron mines, as well as ships to bring the raw materials to his railroad, which brought it to his iron and steel works, which turned out the sheet metal for his car parts (he also made his own glass) in a continuous, controlled flow using belts, hoists, and elevators. Raw materials came in the front door, and finished automobiles rolled out the back door and onto Ford's railroad cars and out to the nation. The world beat a path to Henry Ford's door and left on wheels.

BILL GATES

Just as Henry Ford was keenly interested in machines at a time when a new machine—the automobile—was in its infancy, Bill Gates was fascinated by a new machine—the computer—in its early years. Both men became very rich very fast. But that's where the likenesses end.

If Bill Gates was in elementary school today, kids would probably call him a nerd. In the early 1960s, when he was nine years old, the common term was "geek" where he lived in Seattle.

Born October 28, 1955, into a prosperous family with inherited wealth, William Henry Gates III was small for his age. He was high-strung, wore glasses, preferred crunching numbers to batting a baseball, and would rather sit alone in his bedroom thinking than play outside.

When he got excited about a difficult question or a complex answer, he would shout and start rocking. Even today, when standing or sitting, he rocks back and forth while his mind is working, racing with excitement. Bill was a math whiz who would later make a perfect score on his math SATs. His room was a mess, but his mind was clearly focused on two things: computers and how to make money with them.

The computer industry is no older than Bill Gates. The first mass-produced, commercial computer, called Univac 1, was introduced just before he was born. It consisted of vacuum tubes, and filled an entire room. Wild-eyed engineers made fantastic predictions that future computers "may have only 1,000 vacuum tubes and perhaps weigh only one and a half tons."

Starting in seventh grade, Bill Gates attended a private school, Lakeside. There he found a kindred spirit in Kent Evans. They talked the same language and shared the same obsessions: business and computers. Lakeside was one of the few schools that had a computer hookup at that time. Using a teletype machine, the school was linked with a large mainframe housed in downtown Seattle. The school paid a fee for the computer time it used. Once Bill and his friends discovered it, nobody could keep them away from it. They used up a year's budget in a few weeks.

With two older students, Paul Allen and Rick Weiland, Bill and Kent went into business. (Kent was later killed in a mountain climbing accident; the other two eventually worked with Gates at Microsoft.) They called themselves

Fate or Chance?

Being born at a time of great change, be it technological or social, can be an important factor in an individual's success. That was true of Henry Ford and Bill Gates.
  As Shakespeare wrote:
    "There is a tide in the affairs of men,
     Which, taken at the flood, leads on to fortune. . ."
                                                    Julius Caesar

Bill Gates poses next to a computer running his operating software, Microsoft Windows.

the Lakeside Programmers Club, and worked out the school's schedules for the year. They hired an engineer to build their own computer.

Bill spent hours at the downtown computer center, studying the **software,** figuring out how to find the bugs in it and how to make it easier to operate. Afternoons, nights, weekends—that was where he could be found. His obsession with computers gradually narrowed to creating the operating software.

In 1973 Bill went to Harvard; Paul was working in nearby Boston. They continued to bat software ideas back and forth. Then a major breakthrough occurred: a company called MITS came out with the first personal computer, the Altair 8800, a box with toggle switches and no keyboard or

This is what computers looked like in 1946, nine years before Bill Gates was born. Called Eniac (Electronic Numerical Integrator and Computer), it weighed 30 tons and filled an entire room at the University of Pennsylvania.

screen. It was just a kit; the buyer had to put it together. It had no software. Thousands of people bought the computer kit anyhow.

Bill Gates and Paul Allen saw an opportunity. Somebody had to write the software. They were not alone. There were many bright, energetic young computer enthusiasts all over the country who wanted to write Altair's software for these computers.

MITS was located in Albuquerque, New Mexico. Bill and Paul told the company's owner that they had just the right BASIC language program for his computer. He said he wanted to see it. Now they had to write it. For two months they worked day and night, then Allen flew to Albuquerque for the big test. Using their program, could the computer add two and two? It could, and it came up with the right answer.

Bill and Paul decided not to sell their program. They licensed it, collecting royalties on each sale. Bill dropped out of Harvard and they moved to Albuquerque. They formed a partnership, combining the words microcomputer and software to call their business Micro-Soft (later the hyphen was dropped). They designed and licensed software for companies like Radio Shack and Apple. In 1978 Bill Gates and Microsoft returned home to the Seattle area.

Two years later they reached the big leagues. Industry leader IBM was going to come out with desktop personal computers. They wanted Microsoft to do the programming. Working in absolute secrecy for a year, Microsoft developed what's now known as MS-DOS; in 1981 the IBM PC with Microsoft MS-DOS hit the market.

In the computer boom that followed, Microsoft became so successful, its stock created millionaires of hundreds of the company's managers and employees, and it made a multibillionaire of Bill Gates. Microsoft's Windows series was so dominant in its field, the federal government brought an antitrust suit against them, seeking to break up the company.

These revolutionary changes didn't happen overnight. Microsoft Network, a new way to tap into the Internet market and combine it with Windows, took three years to develop.

With all his wealth, where was Bill Gates when he turned 45 in 2000? Not in his enormous mansion near Microsoft headquarters, counting his money. He was brainstorming with his engineers, thinking and rocking and yelling out ideas to beat the next challenge he had set for himself: building a better mousetrap by creating software that would enable the user to interact with websites.

Warren Buffett's fascination with numbers led to the creation of a business empire that owns many different kinds of businesses, from insurance and bricks to candy manufacturers and the licensing and servicing of Dairy Queen fast food stands like this one. There's nothing new or exciting or high tech about them. They just make money for Buffett and his investors.

The Money Makers

WARREN BUFFET

Nobody can explain how or why someone is born with a particular talent or interest. Warren Buffet was born on August 30, 1930, in Omaha, Nebraska, with a fascination for numbers. He had a mind that could record and remember all sorts of numbers from populations to timetables. He filled notebooks with traffic counts to baseball **statistics,** and studied them for hours at a time, looking for trends, patterns, meanings.

He looked for ways to make a few dollars, not just odd jobs but businesses. He retrieved and sold golf balls that had been lost in the woods around golf courses. He compared racetrack odds with horses' records, picked winners, and tried to sell his advice. He set up lemonade stands, but only after studying the traffic counts at different locations. He vowed to become a millionaire by the age of 30. And he did all this before he was 10 years old.

In 1942 his father was elected to Congress and the family moved to northern Virginia. While in high school, Warren delivered newspapers, and built that into a business with five routes for two newspapers. He took some of his earnings and bought farmland in Nebraska. He was 14.

In college Warren could memorize whatever he read or heard in a lecture. He didn't have to study to get by. But he didn't think he was learning much, either. Then he went to Columbia University in New York, where he met the man who became his mentor, Benjamin Graham.

The place where numbers and money come together with the greatest profit potential is the stock market. Graham taught Warren how to apply his love and understanding of numbers and mathematics to analyzing a company. Using the principles in Graham's book, *The Intelligent Investor,* Warren learned how to figure out if a company's stock was cheap, dirt cheap, a real bargain—or not.

Warren understood the difference between something being frequently correct and something that was always correct. He realized that the stock market frequently priced stocks in line with their value, but not always. It was the exceptions that he would seek out.

There is no right or proper price for the stock of any company. The marketplace of buyers and sellers may roughly agree on the value of most companies at any given time. It didn't matter to Warren if the prices of 50,000 stocks were "about right" in most people's minds. He was interested in finding the few he thought were worth much more than

Warren Buffett ignored all the methods used by most professional money managers, and made millions for himself and his investors. The stock of his company, Berkshire Hathaway, is the highest priced stock on the New York Stock Exchange.

their selling price. He would then buy them, and when the rest of the world discovered them and bought them, they would make him rich.

In 1956 Warren went back to Omaha and began his business of managing money. He was 26. His family and friends invested $105,000 with him. He was not interested in trading stocks. He was investing in businesses, not stocks. The shares of common stock were just the means for owning a piece of the business itself. He took a long-term view, and was willing to hold an investment for decades if the company continued to prosper and grow.

Warren found the bargains he was looking for. He soon attracted more and more money to manage. He remained a faithful disciple of the investing principles of Benjamin Graham. He ignored what other Wall Street analysts and commentators were saying. He was immune from the emotional roller coaster that most people rode in the stock market, and used other people's extremes of greed and fear to his advantage.

"I will tell you the secret of getting rich on Wall Street," he said. "You try to be greedy when others are fearful and you try to be very fearful when others are greedy."

Warren made everyone who stayed with him enormously wealthy, and amassed a personal fortune exceeding $10 billion. In 1995 he became the wealthiest man in America. He enjoyed the recognition and acclaim he earned for what he did, but he remained a down-to-earth Midwesterner. He could buy anything he wanted, but he didn't want much. If he had a dollar bill in his hand, he was more likely to calculate what it would be worth in 20 years than to spend it. He lived and worked in a modest home on an ordinary street in Omaha. He had a private jet, but would just as soon

Berkshire Hathaway

The holding company that Warren Buffet manages is called Berkshire Hathaway. Its Class A shares, the highest priced stock on the New York Stock Exchange, have varied between $60,000 and $80,000 a share in recent years. Class B shares, representing one-thirtieth of a Class A share, are also traded.

Berkshire Hathaway's holdings include partial or full ownership of more than 50 businesses, including everything from Dairy Queen to World Book Encyclopedias.

be at home, studying numbers and stock prices, as any-where else in the world.

What drives Warren Buffet and other entrepreneurs and investors is often not greed, not the piling up of more and more money they will never be able to spend. It is the challenge of discovering a bargain by analyzing and under-standing a company: what it does, what it owns, how well it is managed, what it might be worth someday. If his num-ber crunching tells him it's a bargain, Warren might buy the whole company.

Warren Buffett is not lucky because he has made a lot of money. He is lucky because he found his life's work at an early age and 45 years later he was still enjoying it. In an annual report to the stockholders of his company, Berkshire Hathaway, the 70-year-old Buffett said, "I love running Berkshire, and if enjoying life promises longevity, **Methuselah**'s record is in jeopardy."

HETTY GREEN

The United States in the 19th century was a land filled with opportunities to become wealthy. The new Industrial Age saw the beginning of the railroad, oil, copper, silver, and gold mining, and the iron, steel, aluminum, automo-bile, and telephone industries. They required vast amounts of money to build and develop. Both the builders who used the money and the investors who provided it made huge fortunes. Many of their family names are familiar today through the activities of their descendants or the founda-tions they endowed to give away money to worthy causes: Mellon, Carnegie, Morgan, Rockefeller, Ford, Vanderbilt, to name a few.

This era in American history also spawned a host of color-ful characters. Not all the financiers and **tycoons** were nice people. Not all were honest. They routinely tried to out-maneuver, out plunder, out cheat, and ruin each other. Their tactics inspired such labels as **buccaneers** and **robber barons.** Laws were sketchy, regulations nonexistent, the frontier wide open with few lawmen to interfere.

Their ranks included John "Bet a Million" Gates, who made his money selling fence wire in the west, wore diamond-studded suspenders, and offered to bet a million dollars on a horse race; Big Jim Fisk and Jay Gould, a pair of unscrupulous swindlers who once touched off a speculative fever in gold that, when it was over, left Gould with millions in profits and his double-crossed partner, Fisk, wiped out; and Diamond Jim Brady, a super salesman of railroad equipment who could eat enough at one meal to feed a family of four for a week. But none of the financiers of the time was more eccentric than Hetty Green, the richest woman in the world when she died.

Hetty Green was born on November 21, 1835, with an ambition to accumulate as much money as she could and spend as little of it as possible. Her family was wealthy from a fleet of whaling ships based in New Bedford, Massachusetts. Hetty learned everything she wanted to know about making money from her father. In the evening she would sit on his lap while he read the stock market news to her. The financial pages of the newspaper were her picture books.

Hetty grew into a tall, attractive young woman who didn't care how she looked, didn't like anybody, had no friends, and didn't give a hoot. Hetty was an only child and she inherited her father's entire $6 million estate in 1865 when she was 29. That wasn't enough for her. Her aunt died, leaving most of her money to charities and other people, and only about a million in a trust for Hetty, who wanted it

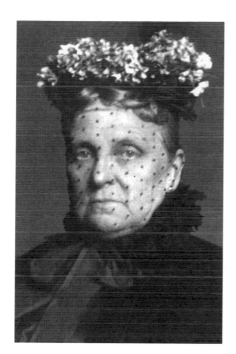

Hetty Green made dollars by the millions and spent them by the penny. The wealthiest and most miserly woman of her time, she was probably never any happier than she looks in this rare photo, wearing a hat and veil.

all. Hetty went to court to break the will. The case lasted five years. Hetty lost.

In 1867 Hetty married a millionaire, Edward Green. They had two children, Ned and Sylvia. The couple split up about six years later and lived apart most of the time. Green died in 1902. Neither of the children liked their mother.

Keeping her own counsel, Hetty Green invested in stocks, bonds, real estate, and railroads. She was a canny, shrewd investor, tough as nails. She refused to panic when prices fell and others around her were selling, and she reaped the rewards when prices went back up.

Hetty Green built a fortune and kept it. She lived by the rule "A penny saved is a penny earned," literally one penny at a time. She wangled free office space from the bank where she had her accounts. She fought over paying every-body from lawyers to maids. She and the children lived in tiny, cheap furnished apartments and moved frequently to prevent people from knowing where she lived. She carried crackers in her pocket to avoid going into restaurants when she was hungry, took her leftover oatmeal from breakfast to the office where she heated it on the radiator for lunch. In the summer, when the heat was turned off, she ate her oatmeal cold.

Hetty Green didn't care if she ever washed, or if her clothes were dirty or frayed. If a dress was torn, she used a safety pin to hold it together. Her son had a muscular

What Became of Hetty Green's Fortune?

Most of Hetty Green's fortune was left in 10-year trusts for her son, Ned, and daughter, Sylvia. When the 10 years were up in 1926, each of them received about $60 million. When Ned died, Sylvia inherited part of his fortune.

Sylvia had none of her mother's financial brains, and kept all her millions in a checking account that earned no interest. She died in 1951 at age 80. Her lawyers knew she had signed a will, but they couldn't find it. They searched every inch of her New York apartment and several houses for three months. One day one of the searchers opened an old tin kitchen cabinet that they had looked in a dozen times before. He stared at the same pile of old cakes of soap they had looked at before. This time he picked them up. There was the will.

Hetty Green's fortune scattered like leaves in an autumn wind. Sylvia left most of it to wealthy people, schools, and institutions who didn't need it, with a little going to hospitals, welfare agencies, and other institutions that did need it. No foundations, memorials, plaques, or buildings bear the name of Hetty Green. Her story is her only legacy.

problem with one of his legs. She refused to spend any money on doctors for Ned. As a result, his leg was eventually amputated.

When she was 59, she had a painful swelling in her thigh. She jammed a stick against it, held in place by her underwear, and walked around like that for 20 years. Finally, when she was 79, she went to a doctor. He urged her to have an operation. She asked him how much it would cost. He said, "One hundred fifty dollars." She picked up her stick and walked out. She was worth about $150 million (about $2 billion today).

Hetty Green died of a stroke at the age of 80. She was buried alongside her father in Bellows Falls, Vermont. A Boston newspaper wrote:

> Hetty Green, who lived as a poor woman lives, and moved from one place to another in order to dodge those who pestered her with appeals for aid, was unable to take her immense fortune with her when she quit this world for the next. She may have thought, when she was earnestly and painfully accumulating her millions, that she could do what no male or female miser before her had been able to do, but she went, and her fortune remained.

The successful people whose lives you read about in this book had very different personalities. They succeeded in different kinds of careers. But they all had the traits that often lead to success: ideas, a clear goal, self-confidence, drive, discipline, and perseverance. Their stories are not unique; many other people have had what it takes to pursue a dream successfully. Many more will do so in the future.

Animated Cartoon—a series of drawings, each one slightly different, that create the appearance of motion when seen in rapid sequence

Assembly line—a system for manufacturing in which each worker adds a part to the product as it passes on a conveyor belt

Buccaneer—an unscrupulous adventurer in business

Capitalism—an economic system in which people, rather than the government, own and operate businesses

Catalog—a publication advertising merchandise offered for sale and shipped to the buyer

Entrepreneur—someone who turns an idea into a business, usually risking his or her own money

Franchise—a license granted by a business to someone to operate a branch of that business in a specified territory

Markup—the difference between what a merchant pays for something and what he sells it for

Methuselah—a Biblical character said to have lived 969 years

Robber barons—businessmen in late 19th century America who became wealthy using illegal or unethical means

Software—the instructions programmed into a computer that enable it to do what you ask it to do

Statistics—numbers collected, classified, and studied in search of standards, patterns, or answers to problems

Stock—a share in the ownership of a corporation, represented by a certificate

Tycoon—someone of great wealth and power in the business world

Boyd, Aaron. *Smart Money: The Story of Bill Gates.* Greensboro, North Carolina: Morgan Reynolds, 1995.

Brands, H. W. *Masters of Enterprise.* New York: The Free Press, 1999.

Dickinson, Joan D. *Bill Gates.* Springfield, New Jersey: Enslow Publishers, Inc., 1997.

Fanning, Jim. *Walt Disney.* Broomall, Pennsylvania: Chelsea House Publishers, 1994.

Gelderman, Carol W. *Henry Ford: The Wayward Capitalist.* New York: Dial Press, 1981.

Trimble, Vance H. *Sam Walton.* New York: Dutton, 1990.

NORMAN L. MACHT is the author of more than 30 books, many of them biographies for Chelsea House Publishers. He is the president of Choptank Syndicate, Inc. and lives in Easton, Maryland.